HOW TO DRAW FUNNY FACES

**Illustrated by
Karen Walker**

**MALLARD
PRESS**

An Imprint of BDD Promotional Book Company, Inc.
666 Fifth Avenue
New York, N.Y. 10103

Mallard Press and its accompanying design and logo
are trademarks of BDD Promotional Book Company, Inc.

Copyright © 1991 Kidsbooks Inc.

First published in the United States of America
in 1991 by The Mallard Press

ISBN 0-7924-5569-X

Introduction

This book will show you some easy ways to draw lots of different funny faces. Some may be more difficult than others, but if you follow along, step-by-step, you'll soon be able to draw any funny face you wish.

Using the basic shapes illustrated below will help you get started. Remember that these shapes, in different sizes and combinations, will change from face to face. Variations of these shapes will also be used.

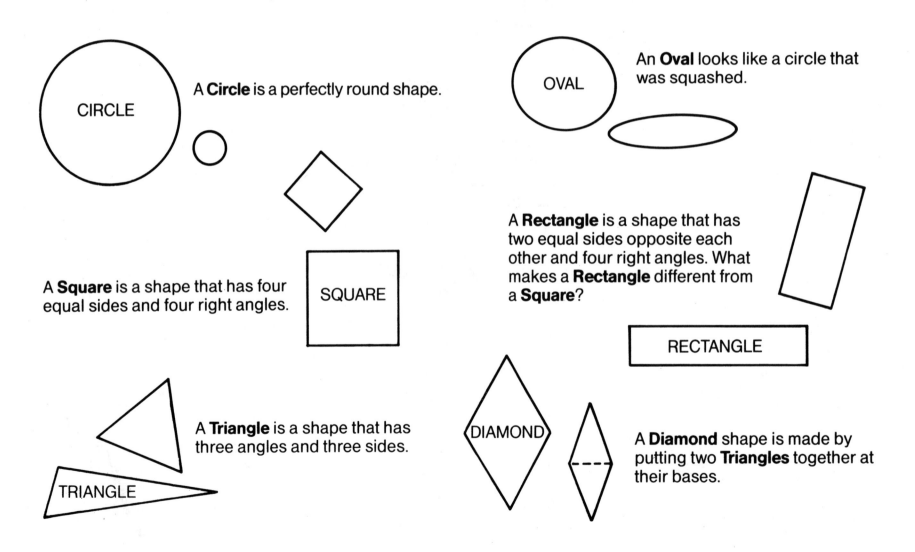

A **Circle** is a perfectly round shape.

An **Oval** looks like a circle that was squashed.

A **Square** is a shape that has four equal sides and four right angles.

A **Rectangle** is a shape that has two equal sides opposite each other and four right angles. What makes a **Rectangle** different from a **Square**?

A **Triangle** is a shape that has three angles and three sides.

A **Diamond** shape is made by putting two **Triangles** together at their bases.

Supplies

NUMBER 2 PENCILS
SOFT ERASER
DRAWING PAD
FELT-TIP PEN
COLORED PENCILS, MARKERS
OR CRAYONS

Helpful Hints:

Before starting your first drawing, you may want to practice tracing the different steps. Start your drawing by lightly sketching out the first step. The first step is very important and should be done carefully. The second step will be sketched over the first one. Next, refine and blend the shapes together, erasing any guidelines you no longer need. Add final details, and when your drawing is complete, go over your pencil lines with a felt-tip pen. If you wish, you may color your drawing with markers, pencils, or crayons.

Each funny face has special characteristics that make it easier or, in some cases, more difficult to draw. However, it's easier to draw anything when you break it down into simple shapes. Remember, practice makes perfect, so keep drawing until you've mastered all of the funny faces. Then, you can use your imagination to create your very own funny faces. Draw scenes featuring two or more funny faces. Experiment with different eyes, ears, hair, glasses, and more! Most of all, HAVE FUN!

Polka Dot Penny

1. Lightly draw an oval, two circles, and a half oval to begin Polka Dot Penny.

2. Add oval guidelines for the hair, and create bow ties with triangles joined by squares. Draw the additional basic shapes as shown.

Remember to erase any guidelines you no longer need.

3. Draw lots of wavy lines for Penny's hair to make it very full. Add the necktie and combine and blend the shapes together.

4. Complete your picture with details and shading, but don't forget the polka dots. Penny would be lost without them!

Zany Zack

1. Lightly draw a large circle for the head, and smaller circles for the ears, eyes, and mouth. Add a square for the neck.

2. Draw two rectangles for Zack's cap. Then, add the additional basic shapes as shown.

Keep erasing and drawing until you are satisfied.

3. Add two smaller circles in opposite directions to form Zany Zack's eyes. Draw his bushy hair with a squiggly line, and curve and blend the rectangular lines to form the cap.

4. Add polka dot details, freckles, and shading. Now Zany Zack looks zanier than ever!

If you like the way Zany looks, polish him off with felt-tip pens or colored pencils. Now you have the perfect picture for your wall.

Ms. Head O'Hair

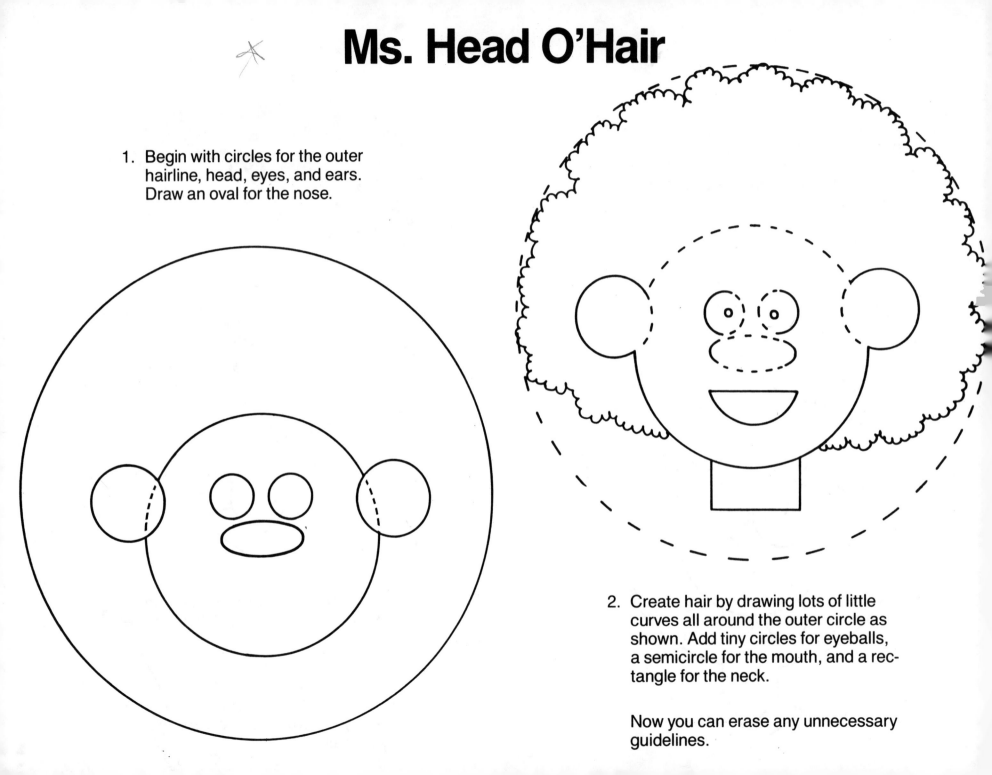

1. Begin with circles for the outer hairline, head, eyes, and ears. Draw an oval for the nose.

2. Create hair by drawing lots of little curves all around the outer circle as shown. Add tiny circles for eyeballs, a semicircle for the mouth, and a rectangle for the neck.

   Now you can erase any unnecessary guidelines.

3. Curve, shape, and blend lips, and add curved lines for the nostrils.

4. Draw lines for teeth, eyes, ears, and eyebrows. Add a flower and other details. Ms. Head O'Hair is now done. But, remember, if you are not satisfied with your drawing, erase it, and begin again. Practice makes perfect.

Laid-Back Larry

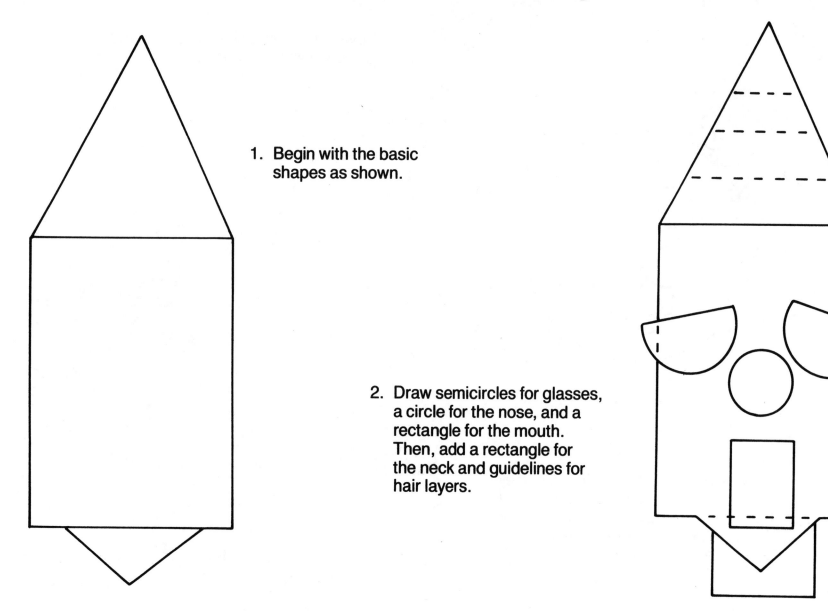

1. Begin with the basic shapes as shown.

2. Draw semicircles for glasses, a circle for the nose, and a rectangle for the mouth. Then, add a rectangle for the neck and guidelines for hair layers.

3. Create Larry's hair with curved, jagged lines. Add a long thin rectangle for the hair band and complete the glasses. Curve and shape the ears, cheeks, chin, and start shaping the mouth.

Hair band

4. Complete the mouth and add lines for teeth. Add the remaining details and shading. Now you have the perfect Laid-Back Larry look.

Mr. Squareface

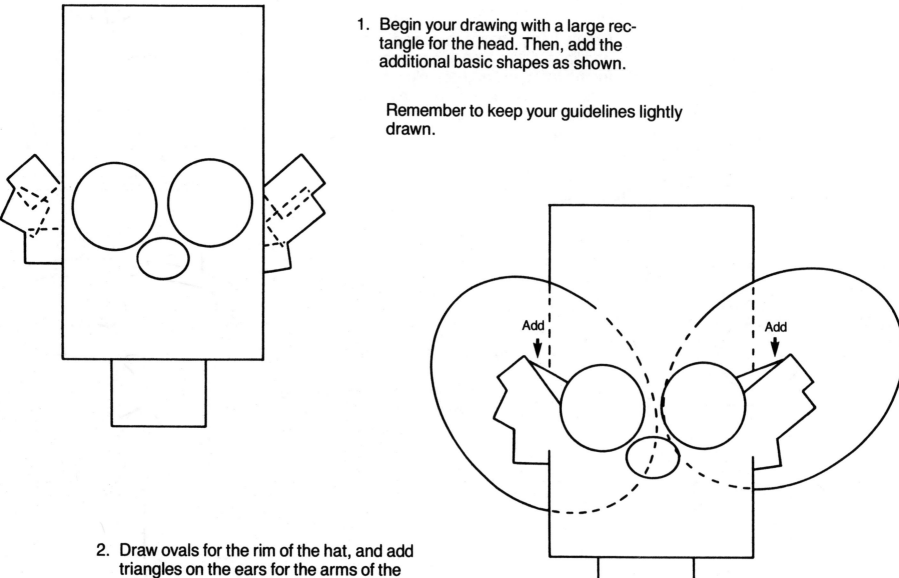

1. Begin your drawing with a large rectangle for the head. Then, add the additional basic shapes as shown.

   Remember to keep your guidelines lightly drawn.

2. Draw ovals for the rim of the hat, and add triangles on the ears for the arms of the glasses. Erase your extra guidelines.

Add

Add

3. Curve and round the top and sides of Mr. Squareface's hat. Create a smile with a curved line and start adding details.

4. Make Mr. Squareface a real square with checkered details and funky hair. Don't forget his freckles.

Funky Fred

1. Start with an oval for the head. Add two small ovals for the ears, and a lightly drawn rectangle to use as a hair guide.

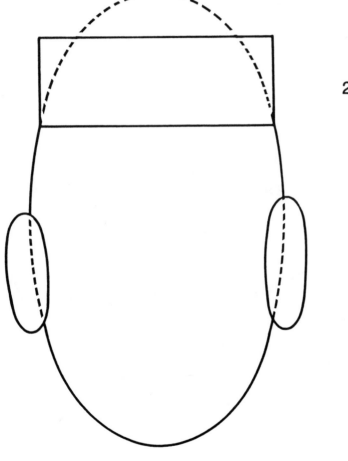

2. Draw two more small ovals, one for each of the top of Fred's ears. Add a small oval for the nose and diamonds for the glasses. Add the neck and two half circles joined together for the mouth as shown.

Hint: Always start your drawings with the largest shape first. Then add the smaller ones.

3. Fill in Fred's hair with lines and dots and curve his face to shape chin. Add half circles for the eyes, tip of the nose, and the bottom lip.

4. Now make Funky Fred even funkier than ever. Add earring, shirt collar, shading, and anything else that's fun.

Note: Erase any guidelines you no longer need.

Star-Spangled Granny

1. Form Granny's head and hair with ovals and a rectangle. Add small squares for her eyeglasses, and a circle for her nose.

2. Draw the headband guidelines and curve Granny's hair with a wavy line all around her head as shown. Her necklace and earring are formed with little circles. Round out the face, lips, and chin.

3. Add details like Granny's headband bow and stars, and curved mouth. Then add shading. Now Granny is set for a star-spangled celebration.

Goggleface Gil

2. Use long curved lines for the hair and shoulders, and two ovals for the collar. Erase any extra guidelines.

1. Start with a lightly drawn oval for the head. Create the eyes, ears, and mouth with circles. Then add a rectangle for the neck and a triangle for the nose.

3. To complete Goggleface Gil, add his mouth, shading, and details as shown.

Krazy Katie

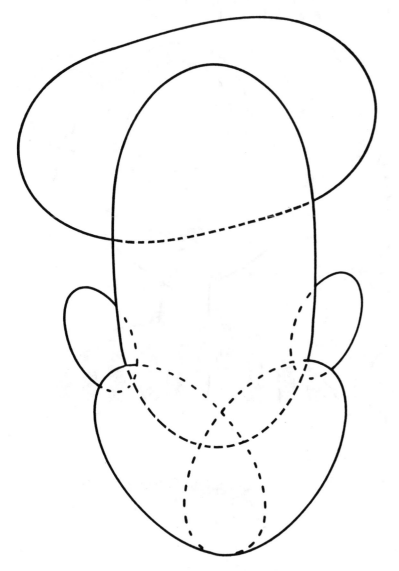

Remember, it's easier to draw anything when you break it down into simple shapes.

1. Begin your drawing with the basic ovals as shown.

2. Add rectangles for the headband, two small circles for the eyes, three small semicircles for the nose, and a large half circle for the mouth.

3. Use jagged lines for Katie's hair so it stands up really crazy. Complete her headband and start adding details.

4. Add lines for Katie's teeth, and complete her eyes and eyebrows. Shade in her lips and headband for an awesome Krazy Katie look.

When you think your drawing is just right, you can complete it with felt-tip pens or colored pencils.

Dodo Donald

1. Start with the basic ovals and circles as shown.

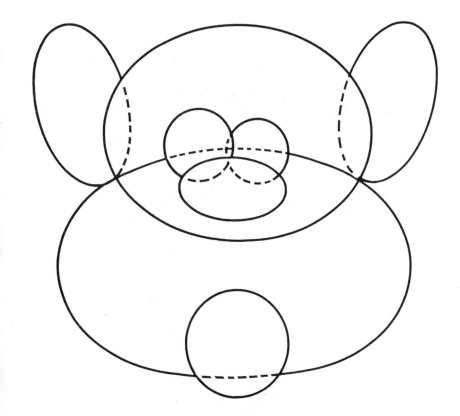

2. Add a rectangle and a square to form the hair guidelines, and a curved line for the mouth. Two straight lines form the neck.

3. Draw curved lines around the eyes and complete the mouth and teeth. Curve the ears and curl the top of the hair. Then blend all the shapes together and erase any remaining guidelines.

4. Add more curved lines, details, and shading to complete Dodo Donald's face. Finally, draw his neckwear with triangles and rectangles.

Screamin' Mimi

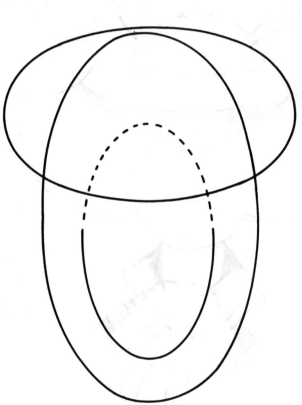

1. Begin your drawing with three large ovals. Remember to draw the largest one first.

2. Draw five circles for the bow, and create two quarter moons for the hair guidelines. Draw a straight line through the center oval to form Mimi's mouth. Then, add a square for her teeth, and a rectangle and two triangles for her neck and collar.

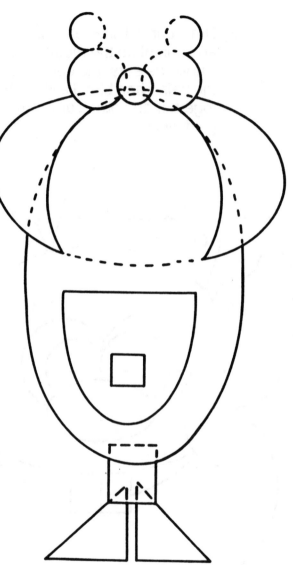

Erase any guidelines that are no longer needed.

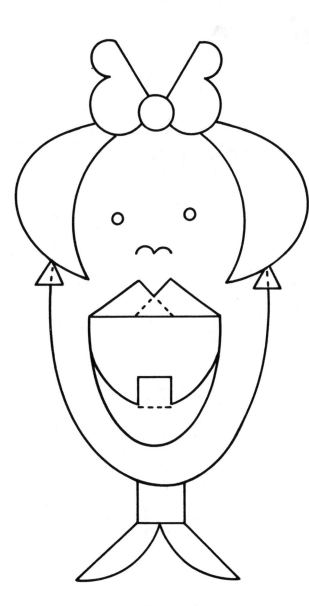

3. Complete the hair bow and draw the additional basic shapes as shown.

4. Add glasses, and the remaining details and shading to get a scream out of Mimi.

Mr. Chucklehead

1. Start your drawing with a long egg-shaped oval. Add additional ovals for the cheeks and ears, and a rectangle for the neck.

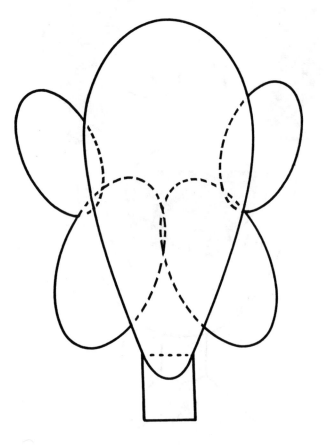

2. Draw long, wavy lines for hair and add circles for the eyes. Draw the nose, mouth, and bow tie using the basic shapes as shown.

3. Add two small circles for eyeballs and two half ovals for
   nostrils. Create the lips and
   draw connected triangles for
   the teeth.

4. Finish your drawing by shading mouth, eyeballs and eyebrows, and bow tie. Then add
   any designs that would make
   Mr. Chucklehead chuckle.

Remember, if you are not happy with any part
of your drawing, erase it and start again.

Honky Tonk Ted

1. Begin your drawing with a large oval for the head and a square for the top of the hat. Several circles and an oval form the nose, and two rectangles form the ear.

2. Draw long, wavy lines for the beard. Blend the nose shapes together and curl the oval to form a nostril. Create the eye with an oval and a circle.

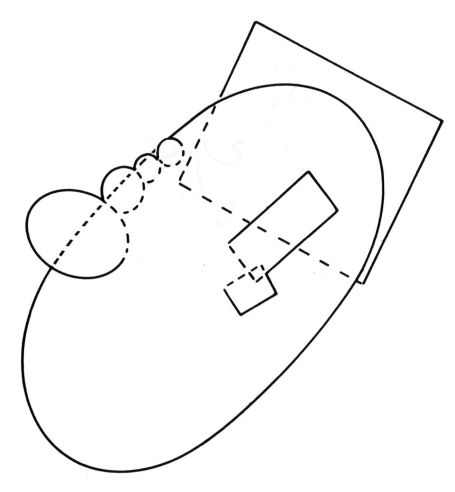

Remember to draw your guidelines lightly, so you can easily erase them later.

3. Add an oval for the front brim of the hat, and a half-moon to form the back brim. Erase any guidelines you no longer need.

4. To complete Honky Tonk Ted, add shading, details, and a flower to his hat.

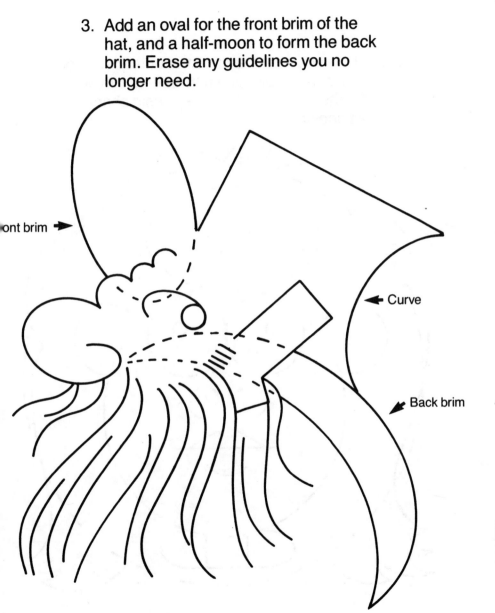

ont brim →

← Curve

← Back brim

Silly Sue

1. Begin with circles for the head, hair, eyes, and ears as shown. Add an oval for the bangs and a straight line for the mouth.

2. Draw wavy lines around the outer circle for Sue's hair. Next, add a three-leaf clover for the nose, and the other basic shapes as shown.

Remember to start your drawing with the largest shape first, then add the smaller ones.

3. Add jagged lines to the bangs and half ovals at the bottom of the nose. Round and curve the lips and mouth, and erase any lines you no longer need.

4. Complete the collar. Then add earrings, other details, shading, and anything else to make Sue look as silly as possible.

Smilin' Satch

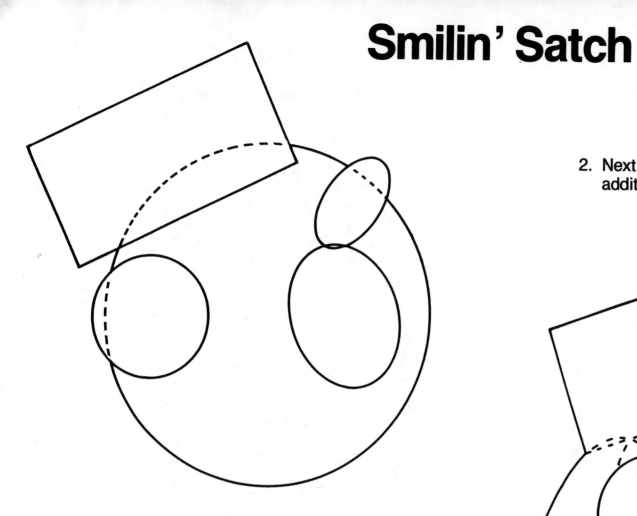

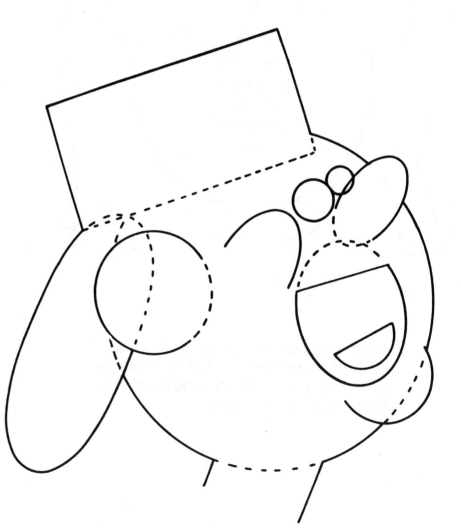

2. Next, add a large oval to the cap and add the additional basic shapes as shown.

1. Begin with a large circle for the head, a smaller circle for the ear, ovals for the nose and mouth, and a rectangle for the cap.

Hint: Remember to draw your guidelines lightly, so that they may be easily erased.

3. Draw a jagged line for Satch's hair, two small circles for eyeballs, and two tiny square teeth. Curve, connect, and blend all the shapes together.

4. Add final details, shading, and lines to finish Smilin' Satch. He's one funny face you won't forget!

Mrs. Fright Face

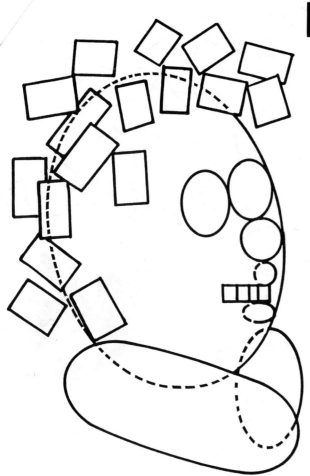

2. Draw a line through each eye oval to form the lids, and add semicircles for eyeballs and nostrils. Blend the shapes to form the nose, mouth, and teeth. Curve the chin and add small curved lines for the furry collar. The ear is formed with various rectangles as shown.

1. Begin with a large oval for the head, and two smaller ones for the collar. Add ovals and circles for the eyes, nose, and lips, and draw small squares for the teeth. Then, add a variety of different-sized squares and rectangles for the curlers.

3. Once you add final details, Mrs. Fright face is sure to frighten everyone!